Cover illustration: British aircraft carriers were home to the Buccaneer strike bomber for nearly two decades. This example, bombed up for a 'shop window' display, is a Mk. 2 from the Fleet Air Arm's last operational unit, No. 809 Squadron, embarked aboard *Ark Royal* from 1970 to 1978. In the background is one of the carrier's two plane guard Wessex HAS.1 helicopters, watching the launch preparations. (HMS *Ark Royal*/FPU)

1. The last front-line role for the Scimitar began in September 1964, when No. 800 Squadron (then operating Buccaneer S.1s) formed a B Flight, comprising Scimitars equipped with American-style 'buddy pack' refuelling pods – which explains the beer mug badge on this aircraft's fin. Note the jet blast deflector and the projector sight landing aid. (RNAS Yeovilton)

WARBIRDS ILLUSTRATED No 33

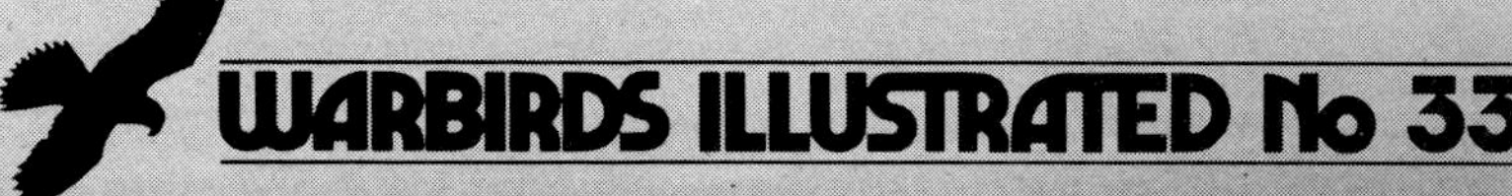

BRITISH NAVAL AIR POWER

1945 to the present

PAUL BEAVER

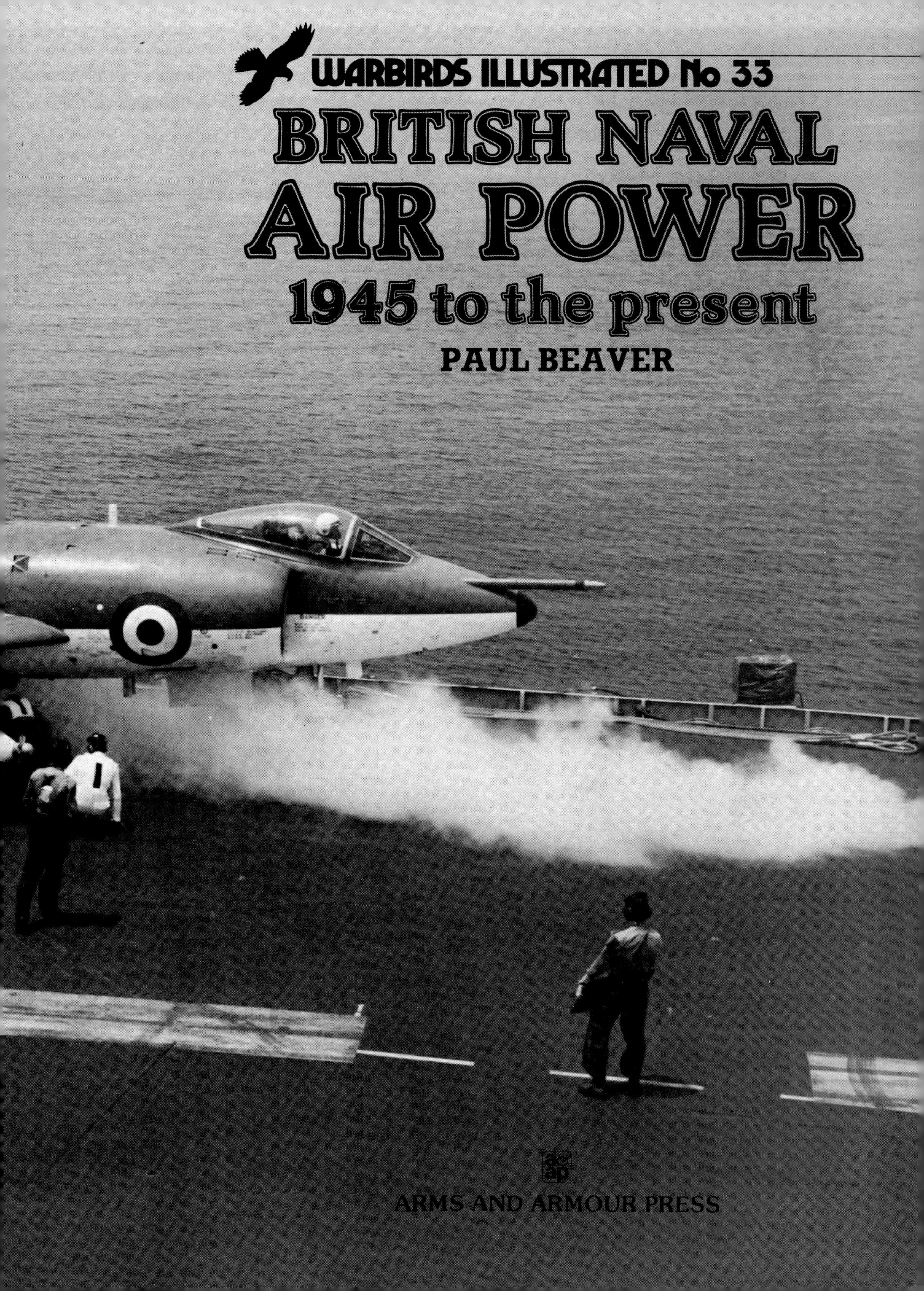

ARMS AND ARMOUR PRESS

XN977
XT271

Introduction

Published in 1985 by Arms and Armour Press
2-6 Hampstead High Street, London NW3 1QQ.

Distributed in the United States by
Sterling Publishing Co. Inc., 2 Park Avenue,
New York, N.Y. 10016.

British Library Cataloguing in Publication Data:
Beaver, Paul
British naval air power, 1945 to the present. – (Warbirds illustrated; v.33)
1. Great Britain. *Royal Navy. Fleet Air Arm.* – History 2. Airplanes, Military – Great Britain – History
I. Title II. Series
623.74'6'0941 UG1245.G7
ISBN 0-85368-710-2

Editing, design and artwork by Roger Chesneau.
Typesetting by Typesetters (Birmingham) Ltd.
Printed and bound in Italy
by Tipolitografia G. Canale & C. S.p.A. - Turin
in association with Keats European Ltd.

It is not often that one is invited to undertake a task which is pure self-indulgence, for that is what this picture album has become. The period from the end of the Second World War to the present day has been one of incredible development, change, success and disappointment for the Royal Navy's Fleet Air Arm, the service which has exercised British naval air power so well. Further, this period is arguably the most interesting and important in the evolution of naval air power and the operational use of naval aircraft. The conflicts that have taken place during the postwar years – Korea, Malaya, Suez, Borneo, 'Confrontation', Aden, the South Atlantic – have shown just how valuable naval aviation is to any country, and especially to a maritime power like Great Britain.

The reintroduction of carrier aviation in the 1980s with the commissioning of three light aircraft carriers – previously termed 'ASW cruisers' – and the entry into service of the Sea Harrier short take-off and vertical landing (STOVL) fighter have given the Fleet Air Arm the basis of its development until the end of the decade. As for helicopters, the Royal Navy already flies some of the best equipment in the world, although there is some doubt about the number of decks which will be available from which to use these valuable assets.

Despite the fact that the Falklands conflict of 1982 has played an important part in shaping the future of British naval air power, this episode has been deliberately under-emphasized in this volume, if only because it is deserving of a picture album all to itself. Similarly, not every British naval aircraft of the past four decades is featured between these covers; those included are representatives of the equipment used to promote naval air power, and photographs have been chosen that are pleasing to the eye. I am most grateful to my friends for the loan of pictures and to the office of Flag Officer Naval Air Command, the Fleet Air Arm Museum, the Royal Air Force Museum, Westland plc and the Fleet Photographic Unit for their considerable assistance. Photographs from naval establishments are Crown Copyright.

Preparing this work in the FAA's 70th Anniversary year, one cannot help looking back on the past decades and thinking of what might have been but for politicians. To a certain extent, that is why there is in this book a concentration on the 1950s and 1960s, when naval aviation was in a prime position. Britain was lucky to have the right sort of people in the Admiralty, in the aircraft, shipbuilding and equipment manufacturing industries and, above all, in the ranks of the Royal Navy. The reader is invited to reflect on the importance of and need for seaborne air power. Other nations are even now improving and re-equipping their naval air arms at a far greater speed than Great Britain. A maritime nation needs maritime air power – Fly Navy!

Paul Beaver

◀2

2. The Blackburn (later Hawker Siddeley) Buccaneer was one of the most effective naval strike aircraft ever designed; although no longer in service with the Royal Navy, it continues to fly with the Royal Air Force. In March 1961, No. 700B Squadron was established as the Intensive Flying Trials Unit at RNAS Lossiemouth, over which station this superb photograph was taken four years later, after the uprated and improved S. Mk. 2s had been delivered. The role of the Buccaneer was conventional anti-shipping or nuclear strike, using a toss-bombing routine. (RN via M. H. Larcombe)

▲3

▲4 ▼5

6▲

3. The immediate post-Second World War period saw the decline of the Fleet Air Arm, but the continued use of wartime aircraft or their derivatives. One such was the Griffon-engined Supermarine Seafire FR.47, the last of the Seafire naval fighters, built by Vickers-Armstrong at Castle Bromwich. (FAA Museum)
4. Although the Lend-Lease aircraft from the United States should have been returned or broken up at the end of the war, several Royal Naval Volunteer Reserve squadrons operated the Chance Vought Corsair IV until August 1946. This is an example from No. 1851 Squadron, embarked on board *Vengeance*. (RNAS Yeovilton)
5. The Fairey Barracuda had a mixed reception when it first entered naval service, yet some aircraft like this Barracuda TBR.3 (modified from a wartime Mk. II) carried out training tasks into the 1950s. (RNAS Yeovilton)
6. Photographed probably aboard *Indomitable*, a Barracuda TBR.3 makes a rolling take-off prior to the launch of a flight of Sea Hornet NF.21 fighters. The latter entered service with No. 809 Squadron in 1949 and first went to sea in 1951.
7. The Sea Hornet F.20 was a development of the Mosquito and stemmed from the requirement to develop a reliable, long-range fleet fighter for such operational areas as the Pacific and Indian Oceans. The aircraft first equipped No. 801 Squadron on board *Implacable* in 1949, and the type was eventually phased out of service in 1955. (FAA Museum)

7▼

▲8 ▼9

8. The writing was on the wall for the piston-engined fighter at sea – or so everyone thought, when the first naval prototype of the Supermarine Attacker landed aboard *Illustrious* in October 1947. The aircraft became, in the 1950s, the Fleet Air Arm's first jet aircraft, but it could never be rated as successful. (RNAS Yeovilton)
9. The 1950s also saw the last of the Royal Navy's piston-engined fighters – the beautiful Hawker Sea Fury, which was credited with 460mph at altitude. Its heyday coincided with the Korean War, and it was even the victor, in a dog-fight, over the MiG-15 jet, but its main role was strike, as illustrated here by Sea Furies on board *Ocean*. (FAA Museum)
10. Amongst the new equipment which came into service during the early 1950s was the helicopter. Although the British had experimented with early American designs in the 1940s, the Westland Dragonfly (a licence-built version of the Sikorsky S.51), for carrier search and rescue, was the Royal Navy's first truly operational helicopter. Note in this photograph the early winch gear and the fact that the 'survivor' is still wearing his naval cap.
11. A fully loaded Sea Fury about to be catapulted into the air from the deck of the light fleet carrier *Theseus* operating off the coast of Korea as part of the United Nations forces. This aircraft is an FB.11, from No. 807 Squadron.

10▲ 11▼

▲12 ▼13

12. The last Sea Fury squadrons were those of the Royal Naval Volunteer Reserve, which was disbanded in 1957, but the Royal Navy keeps one single-seat aircraft for display purposes. It is seen here in the hands of Lt. Cdr. Pete Sheppard, himself a veteran of the period. (RNAS Yeovilton)
13. Not all the Sea Fury's time was spent in hostilities: these aircraft are embarked aboard the fleet carrier *Indomitable* during a visit to Sweden in the summer of 1951. But the days of the piston-engined fighter were numbered, and the age of the jet was dawning.
14. The Sea Fury's partner in the Far East was the Fairey Firefly. This beautiful shot shows the first anti-submarine patrol variant, the AS. Mk. 5, flying by its parent carrier *Ocean* shortly after the end of the Korean War. (RNAS Yeovilton)

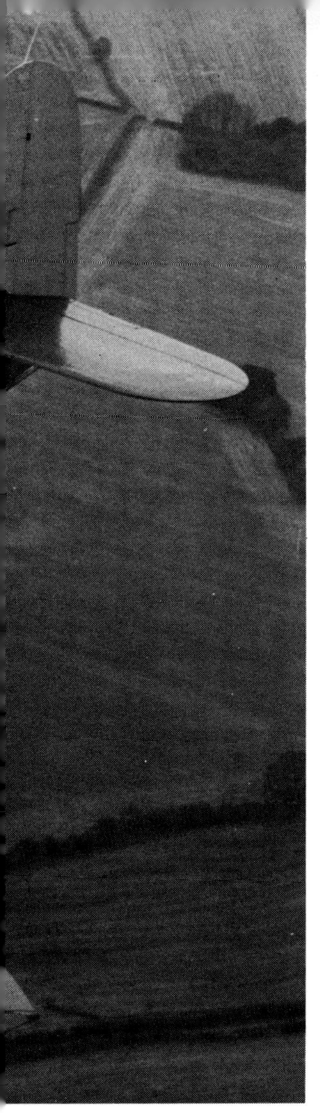

14▲

15▲ 16▼

15. Although the Grumman Avenger served in the wartime Fleet Air Arm and was returned under the terms of Lend-Lease in 1946, delays in the development of the Fairey Gannet brought it back to the Royal Navy. The Avenger AS.4 was supplied to Britain under the terms of the Mutual Defense Assistance Program and served with six front-line squadrons and several RNVR units; this picture shows an aircraft from No. 815 Squadron.

16. Lesser known operators of the Fairey Firefly were the Royal Naval Volunteer Reserve's air divisions – Channel Air Division aircraft are illustrated – which flew from shore bases like Ford but went to sea for annual deck landing training. The carrier here is *Triumph*, and behind the Fireflies are Seafire XVIIs, also rocket-armed for practice firings. (Via Eric Bond)

▲17 ▼18

19▲

17. Another American aircraft to serve under MDAP was the airborne early warning version of the Douglas Skyraider (a type later to see widespread service in Vietnam). The Skyraider was delivered in 1951 and served in AEW flights until 1960, when, like the Avenger, it was replaced by the Gannet. The Skyraider had a crew of three, the two radar operators being seated within the fuselage of the aircraft.
18. All front-line Skyraiders served with No. 849 Squadron, which unit later received the Gannet and the Sea King AEW helicopter. This is a B Flight aircraft operating from *Ark Royal*. (RNAS Yeovilton)
19. In the late 1950s, the typical *Ark Royal* air group included AEW Skyraiders, ASW Gannets, ground attack Sea Hawks and Sea Venom fighters. Again, the two Skyraiders shown are from B Flight of No. 849 Squadron.
20. The 1950s was a period of interesting developments in British naval air power. The Westland Wyvern was born from a 1944 naval requirement for a turboprop-powered strike aircraft but it did not reach squadron service until 1953, going to sea in 1954. The first Wyvern unit was No. 813 Squadron, which embarked on board *Eagle* (tail code 'J') in 1954.
21. A catapult launch for a Wyvern S.4 from No. 831 Squadron, embarked aboard *Ark Royal* in 1957, when the carrier was moored at Devonport. Note the squadron badge on the fin; this was later supplemented by the cartoon character 'Flook' on the nose.

20▼

21▼

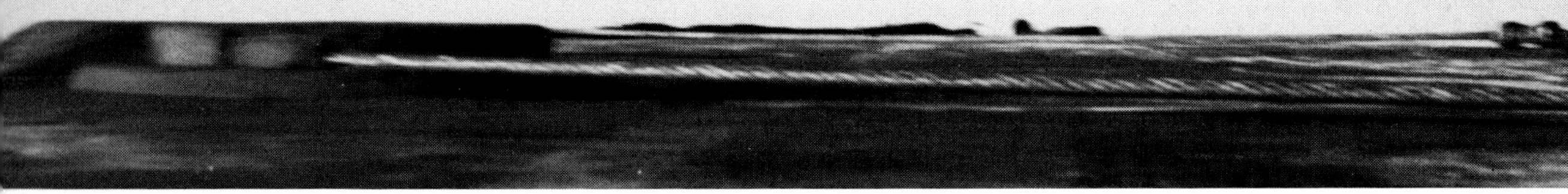

▲22 ▼23

24▲

22. A Wyvern comes in for a 'touch and go' on board *Eagle*, displaying 'Dennis the Menace', whose bomb is marked with the squadron's number, 813. This unit was the last to fly the aircraft, disbanding at RNAS Ford in March 1958. (RNAS Yeovilton)
23. The Fairey Gannet was the world's first turboprop aircraft to land on a flight deck at sea; it was also the first to be fitted with a double-airscrew turbine powerplant, and thus combined the safety and economy associated with conventional twin-engined aircraft with the space-saving advantages of single-engined types. The Gannet AS.1 went to sea in late 1955 with No. 824 Squadron aboard the new fleet carrier *Eagle* (code 'J'), having previously been assigned to *Ark Royal* (code 'O'). (RNAS Yeovilton)

24. No. 824 Squadron flies past the camera and its new home, the fleet carrier *Ark Royal*, October 1955. The Gannet at that time was employed principally as a hunter-killer anti-submarine aircraft, although it could also fulfil a strike role with wing-mounted rockets.
25. In order to qualify aircrew for the Gannet, a dual-control trainer conversion of the AS.1 was built. This is the first prototype T.2, in natural metal finish with yellow bands, the standard scheme for training aircraft of the day. Note the periscope sight, to allow the back-seat instructor to monitor the landing/recovery phases of the student's flight; the third cockpit is unmanned, as was customary with this variant.

25▼

▲26 ▼27

28▲

26. The Gannet at sea. The venue is *Ark Royal*, her deck letter now changed from 'O' to 'R' (hence the washing-out of the 'O' on the flight deck), and the Gannet squadron embarked is No. 815. The carrier is seen leaving Gibraltar.
27. The jet era began for the Fleet Air Arm in 1951, when the first Supermarine Attackers entered service with No. 800 Squadron; the type served until it was replaced by the Sea Hawk in 1954. During this period, the Attacker proved jet carrier-borne operations and took part in the Coronation Review at Spithead. The photograph shows Attacker F.1s from the first production batch, armed with four 20mm cannon. (FAA Museum)

28. The Fairey Firefly, a wartime design, played an important part in the development of British naval air power and allowed the Fleet Air Arm to progress from the straightforward strike role to the more complex task of anti-submarine warfare. This particular Firefly AS.5, painted in the markings of No. 814 Squadron, HMS *Glory* (Korea), is now part of the RN Historic Flight.
29. Britain's first naval aircraft capable of delivering a nuclear weapon was the Supermarine Scimitar, seen here in the markings of No. 803 Squadron, which served with *Ark Royal* and *Hermes* (illustrated) in the early 1960s. Note the nose-high attitude just prior to launch. (RN via Alan Kennedy)

29▼

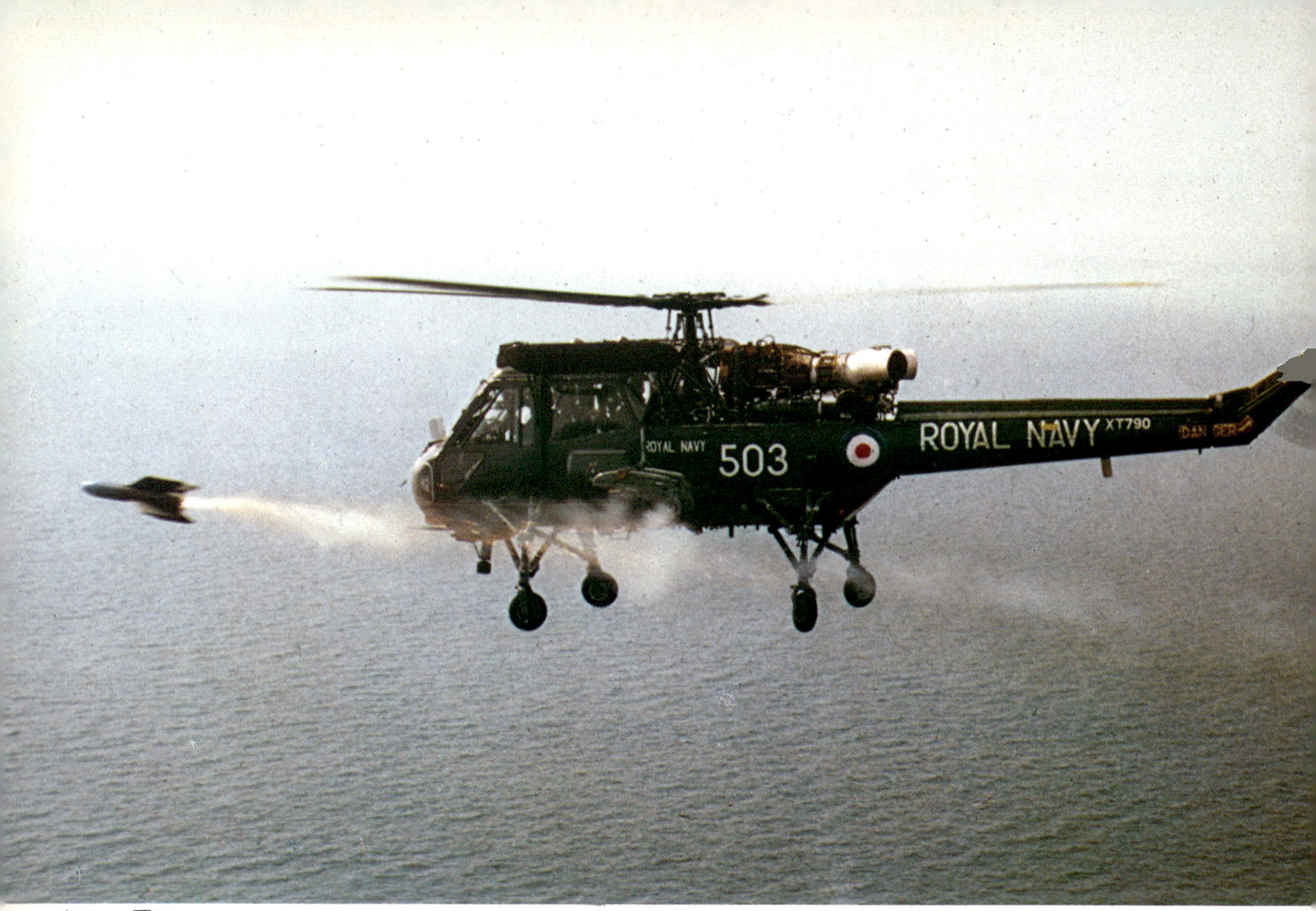

▲30 ▼31

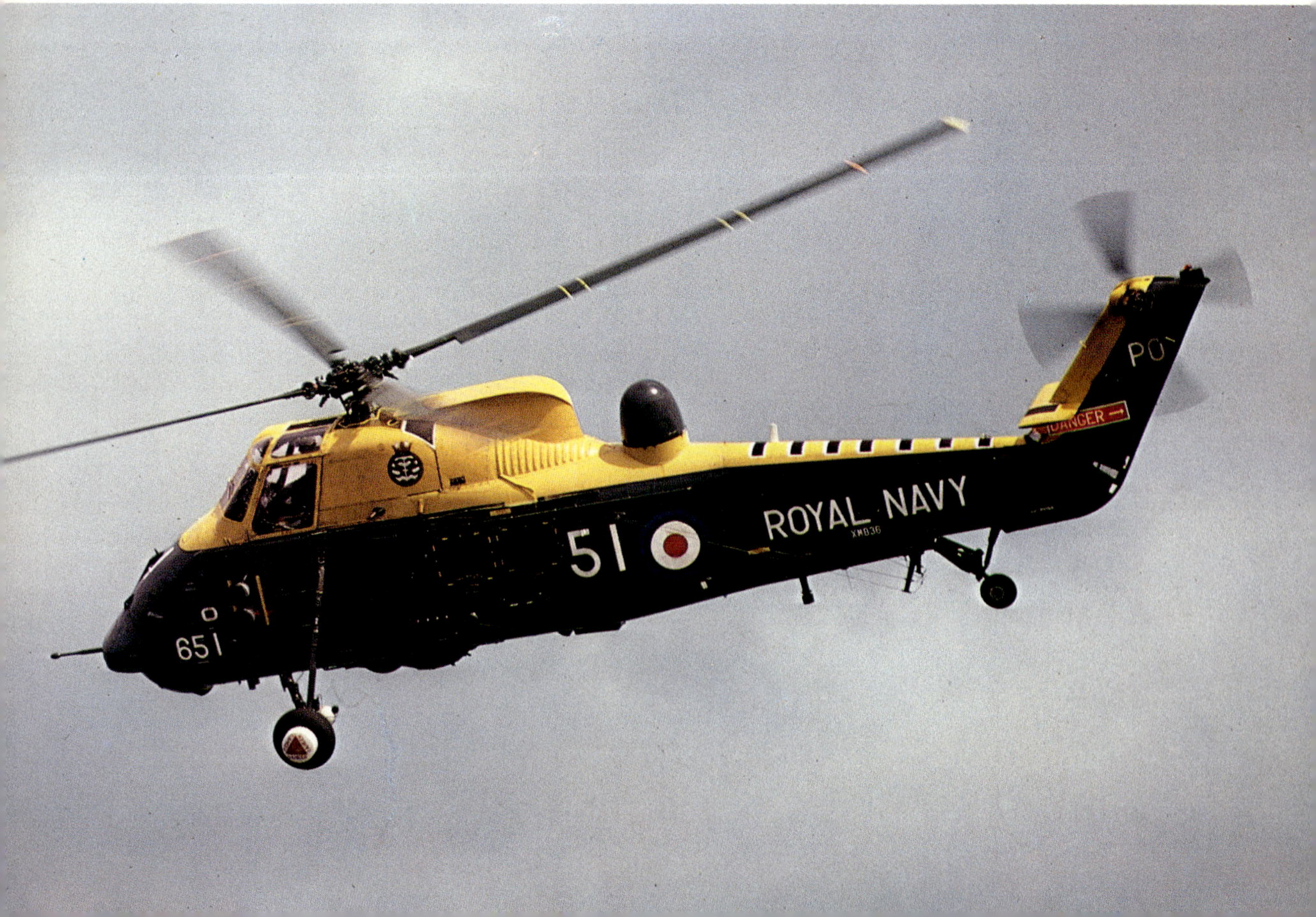

32▲

30. The Westland Wasp brought small-ship helicopter operations to the fore and provided the Fleet Air Arm with a credible ASW platform, away from the parent frigate. In addition, the Wasp was armed with the AS.12 wire-guided missile and it was this combination which assisted in the crippling of the Argentine submarine *Santa Fe* in 1982. (RN photo)
31. A Wessex Mk. 3 painted in the distinctive ASW scheme of yellow and dark blue. The type served aboard destroyers, cruisers and aircraft carriers during its career in the Fleet Air Arm, this particular example flying with No. 737 Squadron, the Portland-based training unit.
32. Over 430 beautiful yet diminutive Hawker Sea Hawk fighters were built for the Royal Navy during the 1950s. These aircraft superseded both the Attacker and the Sea Fury in squadron service, and went to war in 1956 during the Suez crisis. The aircraft pictured is an early production Sea Hawk F.1. (FAA Museum)
33. The Sea Hawk FB.3 was a fighter-bomber version, with strengthened wings to take up to four 500lb bombs. This aircraft, from No. 897 Squadron, was embarked on board *Eagle* during her post-Suez commission in the Mediterranean. (FAA Museum)

33▼

106
XE462
XE386
102
101
XE365
ROYAL NAVY
104
WV805
100
XE342
110

34. Although the FB.3 was the most numerous variant of the Sea Hawk, the FGA.4/6 series was the most popular with aircrew. Because of its good power-to-weight ratio, the Sea Hawk was a superb formation aerobatic platform, as can be judged from this view of No. 800 Squadron (from *Ark Royal*) going through its paces. (FAA Museum)
35. The smaller light fleet carriers were also home for the Sea Hawk, although even this small fighter sometimes found the deck difficult. The example shown is an FGA.4 from No. 801 Squadron aboard *Centaur*; the aircraft has made a normal landing, but without the benefit of its nosewheel!
36. Another light fleet carrier which embarked Sea Hawks was *Bulwark*, and a flight from No. 801 Squadron is pictured in the circuit prior to breaking for landing. Note the screen destroyer, which would also operate as a plane guard during night flying operations. (FAA Museum)
37. Aesthetically pleasing no matter how photographed, the Sea Hawk was an important element of British naval air power in the 1950s, when Fleet Air Arm squadrons had a worldwide policing role. No. 898 Squadron, from *Eagle*, was just such a unit. Note the two distinct paint schemes evident in this photograph. (FAA Museum)
◀34

35▲

36▲ **37▼**

▲38

38. The last Sea Hawk unit was No. 806 Squadron, embarked aboard *Centaur* before being shore-based at RNAS Brawdy until disbandment in December 1960. The squadron insignia was the ace of diamonds, an emblem still borne by the display Sea Hawk FGA.6 flown by the Fleet Air Arm. (RAF Museum)

39. The Fleet Air Arm's first all-weather jet fighter was the De Havilland Sea Venom, the Sea Hawk's partner in many carrier air groups of the late 1950s. The first variant was the FAW.20, which entered service in 1954 and is pictured here at RNAS Ford, equipping No. 894 Squadron, one of the units operational at Suez. (RAF Museum)

40. The next Sea Venom variant was the FAW.21, which featured an uprated engine, improved visibility for the pilot, and American-built radar. One squadron equipped was No. 890 (the first Sea Venom FAW.20 unit), which amalgamated with No. 893 Squadron in 1956, embarking in *Ark Royal*; note No. 890's witch-on-broomstick motif in this photograph, and also the early-style 'bone domes' designed for the protection of deck-landing aircrew. (FAA Museum)

41. Although a carrier air group would normally embark only one squadron of Sea Venoms, exercises with combined squadrons were held regularly. This is *Ark Royal*'s flight deck, showing Sea Venoms from Nos. 893 ('*Ark*') and 891 (*Eagle*) Squadrons during the carrier's second commission.

42. The 1950s were a decade of colourful and imaginative squadron decorations on Fleet Air Arm aircraft, as demonstrated in this photograph of a No. 894 Squadron Sea Venom with its checker-board tip tanks.

▼39

40▲

41▲ 42▼

▲43

▲44 ▼45

43, 44. A photographic sortie for No. 891 Squadron, flying from *Ark Royal* during the carrier's first commission and shakedown cruise in the Mediterranean. The backdrop for photograph 44 is Mount Etna, and the squadron badge depicts the 'Kon-Tiki' symbol of Pacific exploration.
45. Also embarked in *Ark Royal* for a short period was No. 809 Squadron, its Sea Venoms marked with the squadron badge and yellow and black striped tip tanks.
46. The tip tanks were retained when No. 809 served on board *Albion* in 1956, but the fuselage motif is a Phoenix (Firebird), the squadron symbol. This particular Venom has suffered a nosewheel collapse – note the fire retardant foam on deck. (FAA Museum)
47. Using *Centaur*'s twin steam catapults, No. 891 Squadron launches for an exercise. Note the jet-blast screens on the flight deck and the mirror landing aid off the port-side deck edge. Each aircraft carries eight 60lb rockets underwing. (RAF Museum)

46▲ 47▼

▲48 ▼49

50▲

48. The Anglo-French operations to protect the Suez Canal in 1956 provided a happy hunting ground for the Sea Venom. Five squadrons flew missions against Egyptian positions, including No. 891 embarked aboard *Eagle*. Note the yellow and black Suez stripes.

49. Not every mission over Suez was a complete success. One of No. 893's Sea Venoms, also flying from *Eagle*, was damaged by Egyptian anti-aircraft fire but managed to return to the carrier for an emergency landing. Here, the aircraft is being cleared from the deck by the Jumbo crane. Suez proved the carrier air group concept, but sadly the campaign was used by critics as a weapon against further carrier building contracts. (FAA Museum)

50. The Sea Venom was withdrawn from front-line service in December 1960, but several remained flying with Airwork Ltd for Fleet Requirements duties until October 1970. The last RN Sea Venoms were retired by No. 750 Squadron at Lossiemouth; this FAW.22 is one such example. (HMS *Heron*)

51. The final mark of the Sea Venom was the FAW.22, which featured an uprated De Havilland Ghost engine. The first unit to receive the type was No. 894 Squadron (*Eagle*), seen here wearing the famous shark's teeth motif and carrying checkerboard tip tanks Note the Westland Whirlwind plane guard helicopter hovering alongside, ready to aid any accident victim going over the carrier's side. (RNAS Yeovilton)

51▼

▲52

52. Nimble and pleasing as the Sea Hawk was, by 1960 it was rapidly becoming outclassed as a fighter/ground-attack aircraft, and the last front-line squadron disbanded in December of that year. This Sea Hawk FGA.6 from the unit (No. 806 Squadron) was photographed during its last commission aboard *Eagle*. (FAA Museum)
53. A view of the upper and lower hangars in *Eagle*, showing the importance of wing and rotor folding. In the upper hangar are the embarked AEW Gannet flight (849D), the Wessex HAS.1 of No. 820 Squadron and No. 800B Flight's Scimitar tankers; below are the Buccaneers of No. 800 Squadron. (RN via I. K. MacDonald)
54. The Fleet Air Arm entered the nuclear and supersonic age with the Supermarine Scimitar, which joined the Fleet at the end of 1950s. At the 1960 Farnborough Air Show, the Scimitar gained fame in the hands of No. 800 Squadron, whose aircraft had special underwing markings. (Brian M. Service)
55. The squadron, ashore from *Ark Royal*, had previously performed at the Paris Air Show in the spring. Note here the in-flight refuelling probes, which gave greater range even though the aircraft was already capable of, for example, flying from Britain to Malta unrefuelled. (Brian M. Service)

▼53

54▲ 55▼

◀56 57▲

56. The last addition to the Royal Navy's aircraft carrier squadron was *Hermes*, seen here at the beginning of a day's flying. Her embarked aircraft include Gannet AEW.3s (No. 849A Flight), Sea Vixens (No. 893 Squadron) and the plane guard Whirlwind HAR.9 (RN via Lt. Cdr. Alan Kennedy)

57. The Scimitar was also flown by second-line squadrons, such as No. 736 from the Fighter School at Lossiemouth. These three aircraft are from the last production batch in 1960, and the Scimitar would remain in second-line service for at least another ten years. (Brian M. Service)

58. After replacing the Sea Hawk, the Scimitar joined carrier air groups still equipped with the Sea Venom; the combination did not work effectively because of the differences in technology and performance between the two aircraft.

58▼

▲59

▲60 ▼61

59. Fully loaded, the Scimitar weighed about 40,000lb and needed the total assistance of the steam catapult in order to take off, even from refitted carriers like *Ark Royal.* When it came to landing, the aircraft was even more restricted, especially on the smaller carriers like *Hermes.*

60. As a general rule, aircraft embarked on board carriers carry single code letters and shore stations use two-letter designations. This example shows Scimitars of No. 700X Trials Squadron at RNAS Ford ('FD') in 1958. (RAF Museum)

61,62. It was in *Hermes* that trials were conducted to give the Fleet Air Arm a stand-off attack capability by arming the Scimitar with the American Bullpup missile. The unit carrying out the trials was No. 803 Squadron, now embarked in *Hermes.* Note the change in underwing lettering!

63. When the Fleet Air Arm celebrated the 50th anniversary of naval aviation in May 1964, the Fairey Gannet AEW.3 had been in service for four years, providing carrier task groups with 'eyes over the horizon' as had the Skyraider beforehand. These aircraft are from No. 849C Flight (*Ark Royal*). (Richard L. Ward)

62▲ 63▼

▲64

64. The heyday of British naval air power at sea was the early 1960s, for by then the Fleet Air Arm was equipped with the Sea Vixen fighter, the Scimitar strike aircraft, the Wessex ASW helicopter and the Gannet AEW.3 for airborne early warning. This is *Eagle*, steaming in the North Atlantic after her mid-1960s modernization. (I. K. MacDonald)
65. Part of the Fleet Air Arm's great potential in the 1960s was its ability to detect, track and identify possible enemy air and sea contacts 'over the horizon'. The medium for this work was the Fairey (Westland) Gannet AEW.3, seen here in the colours of No. 849 Squadron's B Flight aboard *Victorious*. (RNAS Yeovilton)
66. A Wessex HU.5 from the commando carrier *Bulwark*, using its hook for underslung load-lifting during exercises in the North Sea.
67. The Sea King helicopter has proved to be a jack of all trades and the master of most. Here, an HAS.2A from the RNAS Culdrose-based training unit demonstrates the commando assault capabilities of the ASW variant. Six versions of the Sea King have served with the Royal Navy since 1969.

▼65

66▲ 67▼

▲68 ▼69

68. The main RN fleet fighter of the 1970s was the Phantom FG.1, shown here in the markings of the Royal Navy's only operational squadron, No. 892, whose omega emblem signified the last of the true fixed-wing units. Note the Silver Jubilee markings on the radomes and the two Buccaneers circling behind. (FPU)
69. With the new generation of light aircraft carriers, of which *Invincible* was the first, came the new generation of V/STOL fighters for the Fleet Air Arm. The Sea Harrier FRS.1 was a long time coming but it proved its worth during the South Atlantic campaign. This wintry shot was taken aboard *Hermes* during arctic exercises off northern Norway, and the aircraft belong to No. 800 Squadron.
70. When the Gannet first entered service in 1955, it could hardly have been imagined that the aircraft could be redesigned from the anti-submarine version into an airborne radar aircraft. Most of the work was carried out by Westland, and this AEW example from B Flight is seen crossing the round-down of *Victorious*.
71. *Hermes* was in fact the first carrier to embark the Royal Navy's 'eye in the sky' when C Flight went aboard in July 1960; this Gannet is ready for launch from the steam catapult. Note the Whirlwind HAR.7 alongside, acting as plane guard. (Royal Navy)
72. In order to train and work up flights prior to embarkation, No. 849 Squadron, the only unit to be equipped with the Gannet AEW.3, operated a Headquarters flight from Culdrose, then from Brawdy (in South Wales, and where this picture was taken) and eventually from Culdrose again before the aircraft was phased out of service in 1978. (Royal Navy)

70▲

71▲ 72▼

▲73 ▼74

73. The De Havilland Sea Vixen was the Fleet Air Arm's first swept-wing, two-seat, all-weather fighter and the first British aircraft to be armed with guided missiles as the primary weapon system. In this spectacular view, a Sea Vixen FAW.1 is in fact firing a salvo of 2in rockets, but the aircraft was normally armed with the Firestreak infra-red guided air-to-air missile. The aircraft comes from No. 899 Squadron – 'the bunch with the punch'. (HMS *Heron*)

74. The offset canopy for the Sea Vixen pilot allowed the observer to fit into a 'coal hole' on the starboard side of the aircraft – a position from which it could be difficult to escape in the event of an emergency. The Vixen, loved and at the same time treated with great respect by its crews, was a superb air defence fighter, and gave the Fleet Air Arm an aircraft with better performance than those of most air forces of the day. (RNAS Yeovilton)

75. The first operational Sea Vixen unit was No. 892 Squadron, which embarked in *Ark Royal* in March 1960, having formed ashore the previous year. One of the aircraft is pictured launching from the carrier while four Scimitars from No. 803 Squadron await their turn on the 'cats'.

75▼

▲76

▼77

76–79. The Sea Vixen could be counted on to give 'goofers' watching the day's flying from the upper decks of an aircraft carrier a spectacular performance, but not all flight deck accidents ended as happily as this seemingly disastrous situation on board *Victorious*. With the starboard undercarriage leg gone and the drop tank ruptured, the Sea Vixen slews along the deck (76); as it comes to a halt, the observer has ejected his hatch (77); and within seconds both he and the pilot have abandoned the aircraft (78). The flight deck rescue crew then extinguish all the fires, but the aircraft has made rather a mess of the deck (79)!

78▲ 79▼

80–83. The Sea Vixen FAW.2 could also make spectacular landings! Probably experiencing tail hook problems, this No. 899 Squadron aircraft speeds into *Eagle*'s crash barrier, which successfully retards the aircraft (80), although the bottom steel hawser takes off the starboard undercarriage leg (81). The Sea Vixen slews around as a consequence, showing that it is armed with a Red Top missile on the inboard wing pylon (82). In the final photograph, the aircraft has lost both main landing gears (83) and is being descended on by the flight deck emergency crews, which include two firefighters in their 'fearnought' suits being moved in on a Shorland fork lift truck. The aircrew were unharmed except for shock and bruising, and the aircraft was returned to service after repair. (Via Paul Greenway)

▼80

▼81

82▲ 83▼

▲84

84. The Sea Vixen FAW.2 showed improved range and had provision for Red Top AAMs and for two built-in rocket pods in the forward fuselage. The first FAW.2 entered service in December 1963 and the last squadron (No. 899) disbanded in 1972. (RN via M. H. Larcombe)

85. The size of the Sea Vixen's overwing tanks in the tail boom extension can be seen in this view of one of No. 892 Squadron's aircraft 'bolting' from *Hermes*' deck during a work-up period in the English Channel. (Via Capt. P. McKeown)

86. By the end of the 1960s the Sea Vixen's days were numbered, following the Fleet Air Arm's decision to purchase the McDonnell Douglas Phantom for air defence and fleet air superiority duties. The new aircraft – one of the first is here being shown *Hermes*' deck – was ordered in 1964, but by the time it entered service in 1968, the decision had been taken that the fixed-wing naval air power of the United Kingdom would be disbanded, and in the event only one squadron of Phantoms formed for front-line service. (HMS *Hermes* via M. H. Larcombe)

87. From 1962, the Royal Navy used redundant Royal Air Force airframes for training pilots in ground attack operations prior to their joining front-line squadrons flying Scimitars, Sea Vixens and Buccaneers. The Hunter, a swept-wing aircraft, was well suited for this task and remains in service to this day as part of the Fleet Requirements and Air Direction Unit (FRADU) based at RNAS Yeovilton. The photograph shows one of these Hunters, formerly assigned to a second-line unit at Lossiemouth but now with FRADU. (Malcolm English)

▼85

86▲ 87▼

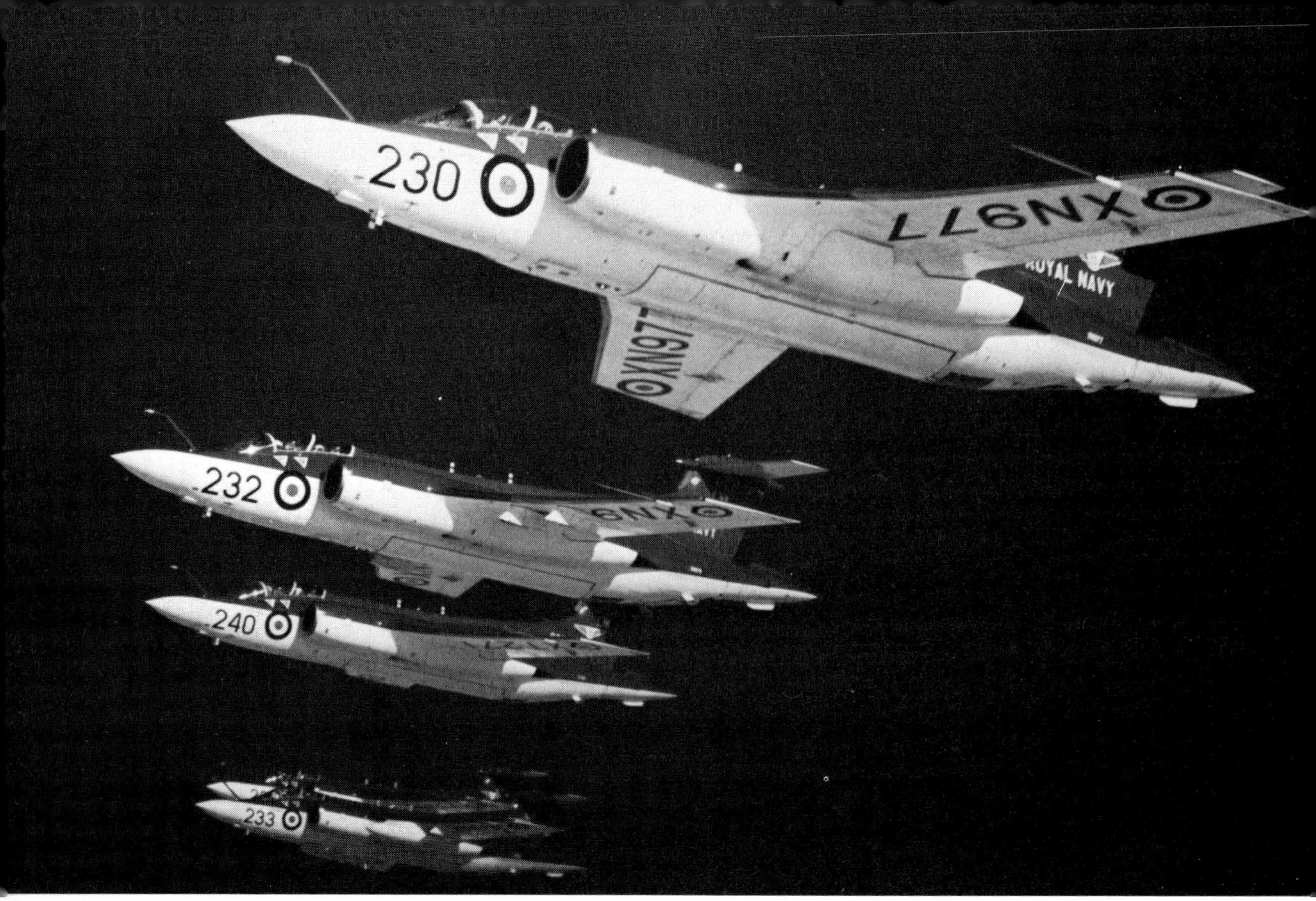

▲88 ▼89

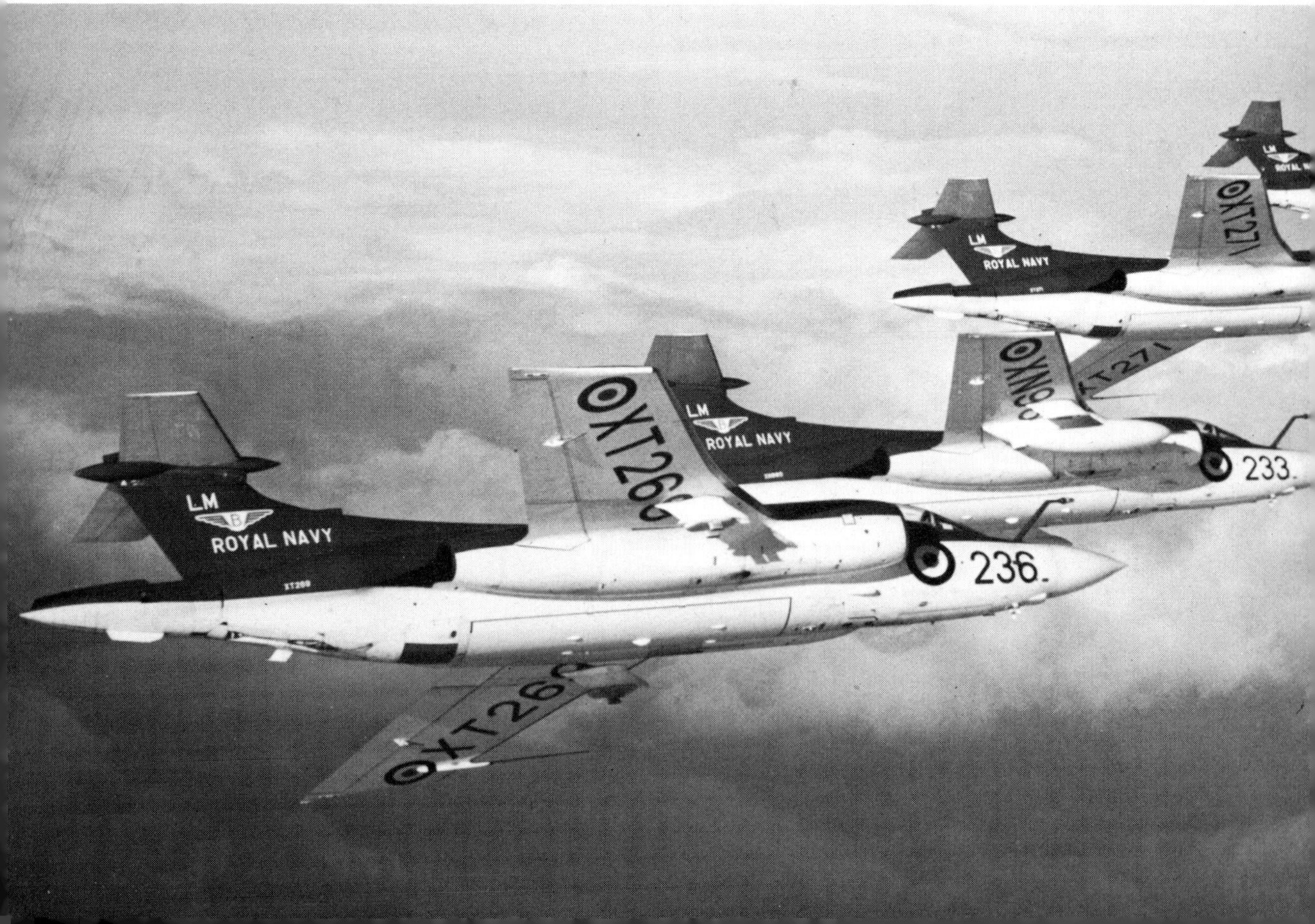

90▲

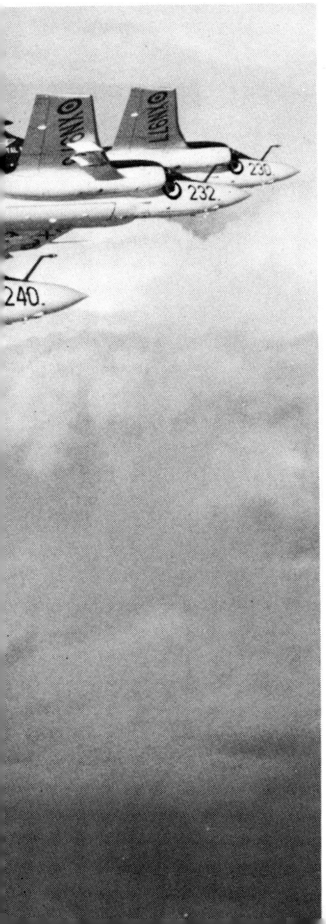

91▲

88, 89. Two photographs showing Buccaneer S.2s over RNAS Lossiemouth (see also photograph 2). Note the characteristic but non-retractable in-flight refuelling probe of the later mark of the Buccaneer. (RN via M. H. Larcombe)
90. Although robust, the Buccaneer could sometimes find itself in trouble, witness here the scene aboard *Eagle* when a Buccaneer from No. 800 Squadron decided to head for a watery grave. Note that the crew ejected just before the aircraft hit the water. (Via I. K. MacDonald)
91. A fine study of a Buccaneer S.2 whistling past the 'goofers' on board *Hermes*. The aircraft is wearing the early dark grey and white colour scheme that was found to be impractical when the aircraft engaged in low-level sorties. (RN via M. H. Larcombe)

▲92

92. When No. 809 Squadron embarked on board *Hermes* for a Far East deployment, the Buccaneers arrived wearing the overall Dark Sea Grey finish that they would retain until the squadron was disbanded in 1978. Note the extended 'clamshell' air brakes and the rugged undercarriage, designed for high landing weights and high-speed touchdowns. (RN)

93. No. 809 Squadron operated in support of British forces in the Aden Protectorate, and three aircraft are pictured here flying near the Crater district of the colony.

94. Later, *Hermes*' air group combined with that of *Victorious* and the Royal Air Force's locally based Hunters to fly past the carrier. The leading aircraft are Sea Vixens; these are followed by twelve Buccaneer S.2s; and the formation is completed by twenty-eight Hunters. (RN via M. H. Larcombe)

▼93

94▶

▲95 ▼96

95. A No. 800 Squadron Buccaneer 'hot to trot', with the ever-watchful Wessex HAR.1 plane guard alongside. In 1967, before this photograph was taken, No. 800 Squadron Buccaneers took part in the destruction of the wrecked oil tanker *Torrey Canyon* off the Cornish coast. Normally embarked aboard *Eagle*, the aircraft were for this operation based at Brawdy. (RNAS Yeovilton)

96. Although the helicopter had already seen service for two decades, it was not until the 1960s that it really made an impact on British naval air power. The first helicopter to do so was the Westland Wessex HAS.1, licence-built from a US design but fitted with a gas turbine powerplant. It entered squadron service in July 1961 with No. 815, and is illustrated here with No. 826 aboard *Hermes*.

97. Although a reliable helicopter, and one which was successfully converted for search and rescue duties, the Wessex was occasionally a casualty in the anti-submarine environment. At least this example from *Eagle* was salvaged, thanks to its flotation bags. (John Keegan)
98. Several ASW Wessexes were converted for use in commando helicopter support duties and operated with No. 845 Squadron in North Borneo in 1963. This is an example from *Albion*, the commando carrier, flying in support of Ghurka troops; note the helicopter's rocket launchers.

97▲ 98▼

▲99 ▼100

101▲

9. A more powerful version of the Wessex entered service in eptember 1967 and was operational for the next seventeen years rom aircraft carriers, guided missile destroyers and shore bases. These two Wessex HAS.3s come from RNAS Portland and are eing recovered aboard the helicopter support ship *Engadine* off the Dorset coast.

00. One technique which enables ASW helicopters to stay in the ir for extended periods is the transfer of fuel from helicopter-apable ships which are too small to recover the larger ypes. The method is known as HIFR (Helicopter In-Flight Refuelling) and is here being practised by a Wessex HAS.3 and the rigate *Rothesay*. (RN)

01. The smaller ASW helicopter also made its debut during the 960s, with the formation of the first Small Ships Flights of Westland Wasp HAS.1s for deployment from frigates. The Wasp, which is still in service, was designed as a weapons carrier which would extend the engagement range of the mother ship; it carries no radar or on-board sonar. (RN)

102. Because of its limited endurance, the Wasp has several important safety features, including the wing-like flotation packs above the cabin. Here, *Ariadne*'s Wasp is pictured refuelling aboard *Ark Royal* during a Joint Maritime Exercise off Scotland. Note the missile-firing sight over the port side of the cabin, used in connection with the AS.12 missiles carried on fuselage-mounted pylons. (HMS *Ark Royal*)

103. (Next spread) By the 1970s, the number of British aircraft carriers had been severely reduced and more emphasis was being put on small-ship naval aviation. Nevertheless, the last conventional carrier, *Ark Royal*, had been refitted and was now capable of operating the Phantom FG.1. Her new air group consisted of Phantoms (No. 892 Squadron), Buccaneer S.2s (809), Gannet AEW.3s (849B Flight) and Sea Kings (824). (HMS *Ark Royal*)

102▼

▲104

104. The other major platform at sea was the commando carrier *Hermes*, capable of operating Wessex HU.5 support and Sea King ASW helicopters as well as carrying a Royal Marines Commando.

105. In the last two decades, the Westland Sea King (a licence-built development of the Sikorsky S-61) has become the most important airborne ASW asset in the Royal Navy, thanks to its ability to detect, track and attack submarine targets well away from the parent ship's task group. This Sea King, from No. 824 Squadron aboard *Ark Royal*, is dropping a Mk. 44 ASW torpedo; an aircrewman is at the door with a smoke float. (HMS *Ark Royal*)

106. The first operational Sea King unit was embarked aboard *Ark Royal*, although No. 814 Squadron (illustrated here over '*Ark*', during the Silver Jubilee Review) was assigned to *Hermes* for much of the 1970s. (Richard L. Ward)

107. The home base for the Sea King squadrons is Culdrose in Cornwall, over which these nine helicopters from No. 826 Squadron are flying. The station, squadron and helicopter have all made a tremendous contribution to British naval air power since the end of the Second World War. (RN)

▼105

106▲ 107▼

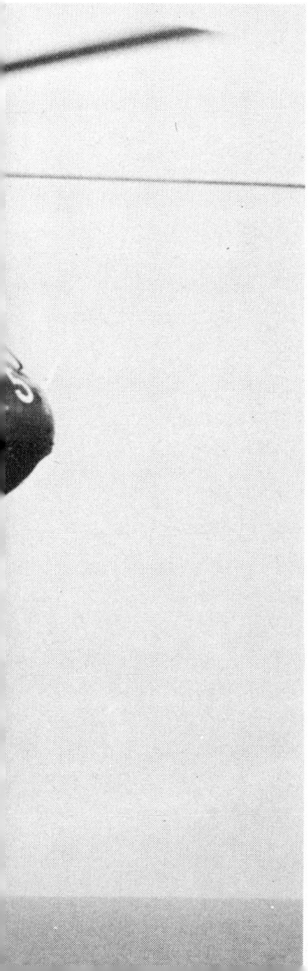

R
ROYAL NAVY
010
024

R
ROYAL NAVY
012

012
PO
ROOKS

◀109

110▲

108. (Previous spread) The McDonnell Douglas Phantom was destined to equip just one front-line squadron in the Fleet Air Arm, No. 892, whose aircraft were assigned to *Ark Royal.* The British Phantom had a characteristic nosewheel extension for launching the aircraft at the correct attitude. Note the blast deflectors – '*Ark*'s deck was specially strengthened to withstand the heat of the Phantom's Spey engines. (HMS *Ark Royal*/L. Air. (Phot.) Pratt)
109. Armed with the acquisition mode Sidewinder missile and equipped with a passive radar warning receiver, the Phantom was part of a force which made the Fleet Air Arm one of the best equipped air arms in the world. This Phantom wears the Silver Jubilee red, white and blue nose decoration and is being fitted with a steam catapult strop before launch. (HMS *Ark Royal*/L. Air. (Phot.) Collinson)
110. The strike element for *Ark Royal* was provided by the Buccaneer S.2s of No. 809 Squadron, one of which is pictured here off the US Navy's Western Atlantic ranges during rocket firing practice. The aircraft could carry thirty-six 2in rockets in four underwing pods. (HMS *Ark Royal*/L. Air. (Phot.) Collinson)
111. *Ark Royal* featured a waist catapult for launching aircraft, and note here the strop falling away to be recovered by a special fitment which allowed for its re-use. Previously, thousands of pounds sterling had been lost annually through the once-only use of launch strops. (HMS *Ark Royal*/L. Air. (Phot.) Collinson)

111▼

▲112 ▼113

112. The venerable Fairey Gannet AEW.3 was frequently first off and last on during air exercises aboard *Ark Royal.* The single pilot can be seen perched above the fuselage which contained the two radar operators/observers and their cathode ray tubes. The airborne search radar was enclosed by the large radome below the fuselage. (HMS *Ark Royal*/FPU)

113. As the use of helicopters from small ships increased, Westland developed an advanced light aircraft capable of surface search (with radar) and of carrying the latest range of naval weaponry. The Westland Lynx HAS.2 entered service in 1976 and played an important role in the establishment of the helicopter in the Royal Navy's inventory. These are No. 700L Squadron machines, aboard the Royal Fleet Auxiliary *Engadine.* (Westland)

114,115,116. The Type 42 destroyer *Birmingham* carried out flight deck trials with the Westland Lynx, equipped with the Harpoon tie-down system, and, as these pictures show, the helicopter is safe even on a rolling platform. (Westland)

114▲

115▲ 116▼

▲117 ▼118

117. The helicopter is used by the Fleet Air Arm not only in maritime duties; it is also employed over the battlefield in support of the Royal Marines. In the mid-1960s, with brushfire wars raging around the world, the Royal Navy received its first twin-engined Wessex HU.5 helicopters – and the same helicopters are destined to remain in service until 1990. Here, a group of RM Reserves awaits collection by a Wessex HU.5 from No. 845 Squadron.
118. The Wessex was first supplemented and then replaced in the commando assault role by the Westland Sea King HC.4, a commando version of the ASW helicopter. The helicopter can lift the 105mm light gun, as shown here at an RNAS Yeovilton Air Day . . .
119. . . . or it can operate in the frozen wastes of arctic Norway in support of the Royal Marines' NATO role. A Sea King from No. 846 Squadron is pictured here landing on a frozen lake, supported by an RM Lynx AH.1.
120. A further development of the Sea King design has been the fitting of Thorn EMI Searchwater airborne early warning radar. Following the deficiency shown in the Falklands conflict by the absence of AEW, this new variant was flying within weeks. The first operational squadron was formed in November 1984 for the Royal Navy's *Invincible* class light aircraft carriers. (Westland)

119▲ 120▼

ROYAL NAVY
F91

◀121

122▲

121. The Royal Navy continues to exercise naval air power for peacekeeping roles in the 1980s; here, the frigate *Brazen* is seen off Lebanon in early 1984. After her patrol in the Eastern Mediterranean, *Brazen* and her Lynx returned home, to be joined by a new pilot, Lt. HRH Prince Andrew. (RN)
122. It took many years for the British Government to appreciate the unique capabilities of the Sea Harrier FRS.1 as a naval fighter and it was the development of the 'ski-jump' principle which spurred them to order the type into squadron service. Here, the first Sea Harrier from No. 800 Squadron makes a vertical landing aboard *Invincible*, watched by another machine from No. 899 Squadron. (RN)
123. The Sea Harrier distinguished itself during the Falklands conflict and has proved a valuable asset to the Fleet Air Arm. In addition to its role as a fleet fighter, it can undertake strike, reconnaissance and surface search duties, and the aircraft equips all three *Invincible* class carriers. This is the CO's aircraft from No. 801 Squadron.

123▼

▲124 ▼125

124. Following the South Atlantic conflict, Sea Harriers and the helicopters of the Fleet Air Arm were painted in toned-down schemes, as illustrated. The main armament of the Sea Harrier is also seen here – AIM-9 Sidewinder AAMs on wing pylons and 30mm Aden cannon pods under the fuselage. (FPU)
125. The Sea Harrier has operated across the world – in the Arctic, in the South Atlantic, in the Mediterranean (as here, during Exercise 'Distant Hammer'), off the United States and in the Far East. It is a versatile aircraft and a proud inheritor of the tradition of British naval air power. (HMS *Illustrious*)